Beasts for the Chase

Beasts for the Chase

POEMS

Monica Ferrell

Winner of the 2007
Kathryn A. Morton Prize in Poetry
Selected by Jane Hirshfield

Sarabande 𝕊 Books
LOUISVILLE, KENTUCKY

With thanks for the G.C.

Managing Editor
Sarabande Books, Inc.
2234 Dundee Road, Suite 200
Louisville, KY 40205

Library of Congress Cataloging-in-Publication Data

Ferrell, Monica.
    Beasts for the chase : poems / by Monica Ferrell ; selected by Jane Hirshfield.
— 1st ed.
        p.   cm.
    "Winner of the 2007 Kathryn A. Morton Prize in Poetry."
    Includes bibliographical references.
    ISBN 978-1-932511-65-9 (pbk. : acid-free paper)
    I. Title.

    PS3606.E7535B43 2008
    811'.6—dc22   2007049509

Cover image: Ruby Osorio, *Sticks and Bows*, 2006, Gouache, ink, colored pencil and
thread on paper, 30 x 22 inches. Courtesy of the artist and Cherry and Martin, Los
Angeles, CA. Image © Ruby Osorio.

Cover and text design by Charles Casey Martin

Manufactured in Canada
This book is printed on acid-free paper.
Sarabande Books is a nonprofit literary organization.

THE KENTUCKY ARTS COUNCIL

The Kentucky Arts Council, a state agency in the Commerce Cabinet,
provides operational support funding for Sarabande Books with state
tax dollars and federal funding from the National Endowment for
the Arts, which believes that a great nation deserves great art.

Contents

PART ONE

PART TWO

PART THREE

Acknowledgments

Grateful acknowledgment is made to the editors of the following publications:

The Canary: "At the White Quay"
Fence: "The Antelope Chase"
Georgia Review: "In the Gabinetti Segretti"
Guernica: "Walking Home," "Harvest"
Gulf Coast: "Myths of the Disappearance" ("I rise like a red balloon...")
The Nation: "The soul is a number moving by itself"
New England Review: "The Fire of Despair," "In the Binary Alleys of the Lion's Virus"
The New York Review of Books: "Knut Hamsun's Night of Fire"
The Paris Review: "Stories from the Tower"
Ploughshares: "Paradise"
PN Review (UK): "Alexander Leaves Babylon," "Mohn des Gedächtnis," "Self-Story as Spheres of Egyptian Industry," "The Blue Grotto"
Post Road: "Echo Digression," "After a Rest: Palimpsest"
Publishing Online: "Sacrifice"
Southwest Review: "Geburt des Monicakinds"
Tin House: "The Lion of St. Jerome," "Eleven Steps to Breaking up a Hart"
Western Humanities Review: "Kaisarion"

"In the Grips of a Sickness Transmitted by Wolves," "The City of Despair," "In the Rain," "Myths of the Disappearance" ("You have stolen..."), and "Herculaneum" appeared as a Verse Press Young American Poets Feature. "Prisoner of the Golden Cage" appeared in audio and electronic format on *Salon*. "In the Binary Alleys of the Lion's Virus" appeared in electronic format on *Poetry Daily*. "In the Rain," "Myths of the Disappearance" ("I rise like a red balloon..."),

"In the Binary Alleys of the Lion's Virus," "Mohn des Gedächtnis," "Alexander Leaves Babylon," "The Fire of Despair," and "The Blue Grotto" appeared in audio and electronic format on *Fishouse*. "The soul is a number. . ." appeared in *Sad Little Breathing Machine* (POL, 2001). "In the Binary Alleys of the Lion's Virus," "The City of Despair," and "The Fire of Despair" appeared in *Asian American Poets: The Next Generation* (Indiana, 2003). "Stories from the Tower" and "Myths of the Disappearance" appeared in *Legitimate Dangers: American Poets of the New Century* (Sarabande Books, 2006). "Mohn des Gedächtnis" appeared in *Language for a New Century: Contemporary Poetry from the Middle East, Asia, and Beyond* (W.W. Norton, 2008). "Walking Home," "In the Binary Alleys of the Lion's Virus," "Mohn des Gedächtnis," "The Fire of Despair," "Alexander Leaves Babylon," "Nighttalking," "In the Gavinetti Sepretti," and "Geburt des Monicakinds" appeared in *The Bloodaxe Book of Contemporary Indian Poets* (Bloodaxe, 2008).

This book began under the guidance of my teachers—Eavan Boland, Lucie Brock-Broido, W. S. Di Piero, Ken Fields, Richard Howard, Marie Howe, and Alice Quinn—thank you. Thanks to Stanford University's Wallace Stegner Program, the MacDowell Colony, the Asian American Writers' Workshop, and the Bread Loaf Writers' Conference for much-needed support, material and otherwise. Thanks to my family for what is beyond enumeration. Thanks to Vijay Seshadri for wisdom and encouragement. Thanks to Jane Hirshfield for her belief in this book, and to Sarah Gorham, Jeffrey Skinner, Nickole Brown, Kirby Gann, and everyone at Sarabande. Thanks to my fellow students over the years and my own students now, whose love of the game inspires me. I owe special debts of gratitude to YiLing Chen-Josephson, Robin Ekiss, and Craig Arnold, for their generous advice on this manuscript, and especially to Cate Marvin and Rick Barot— nothing would have been possible without you two. And thanks to Andrés Colapinto, these poems' first reader; for your loving attention and honesty I shall always consider myself deeply lucky.

Notes on certain poems follow the text.

Foreword

Turn the pages of Monica Ferrell's remarkable debut volume, and the first thing to strike the mind must surely be the immense authority of its intelligence. The second thing, if you are like me, will be something almost the opposite: these pages' fragrance of wildness. And the third? The willingness to enter experience fully, to bear fully its price and brunt. Consider the book's opening, uncompromising lines:

> Tonight the lares have eaten their offerings.
> The sweetbreads are gone, black kidneys
> Infantine and nacred as mollusk-eggs....

These are words not meant for the easily daunted, or for those uncomfortable with the dense accumulation of the world's long knowledge. No reach of mind, or of the senses, is shortened, or shorted, here. With unstinting largesse, *Beasts for the Chase* moves from the funerary miniatures of ancient Egypt to Saint Jerome's companion lion to the Norse gods. And it moves as well with unstinting ambition, in the worthiest sense of that complex term.

If the frontispiece poem, "Harvest," is meant to signal what that ambition consists of, what does it tell us? That the voice will range from objective to subjective without apology. That the autobiographical will be alluded to but not necessarily revealed. That the worlds of archetypal and personal, of mythical and fairy tale, of scientific knowledge and oracle, of Virgil and Plath, will be freely intermingled. That the resulting chorus will have both its dissonance and its wholeness. And that we who harvest, however broadly, are destined also to become the objects of harvest.

This first poem introduces as well Monica Ferrell's Pythian music. The poet speaks here as a sibyl, simultaneously smoke-stunned and sure. Words are malleable, beaten like sheets of silver. "Infantine" stands in place of the more usual "infantile," "nacred" in place of the more usual "nacreous"—an alteration at once condensing and moving the adjective closer to the intimate action of verb. The poem's speaking voice is headlong, both metamorphic and assured in its syntax, and vulnerable. The poet herself, we soon see, becomes the taken offering: "I have made myself so edible, / So extraordinarily meat."

The book moves next to a birth-account, in which Ferrell again weaves the personal into the tapestry of broader cultural inheritance. The title ("Geburt des Monicakinds") adapts a trope from German medieval religious paintings; the modern hospital room is inhabited by the classical gods; inoculation for smallpox— Ferrell was born in New Delhi, into a mixed-heritage family—calls up imperialism in a passing simile. Yet for all its precipitous range, the poem does not forget poetry's essential obligation: not only to think and know, but to think and know through feeling. When smallpox is personified as that which once "put its palm-leaf hand over a quarter of Earth // Saying *these*," the mix of tenderness and adamantine power, the faint echo of the Passover story, the sheer originality of the image both dazzle and chill. Time after time in this collection, the poet accomplishes—seemingly tosses off, at speed—such difficult feats.

American poetry has in recent years entered (or entered in part—to speak of "American Poetry" as if it were a single entity or community would be to be willfully blind) an aesthetic increasingly baroque, one drawing upon rich estrangements as diverse as those of Stevens earlier, Ashbery and Carson now. Too often those who write within this aesthetic allow the worked surface—often genuinely beautiful—to eclipse actual meaning. Too often such books, superficially distinctive, receive notice at the expense of books perhaps quieter of diction but more substantial of thought. In any judging process that involves prescreening—the final judge receives only the smallest percentage of the submitted manuscripts in most competitions, including this one—the judge must wonder if some manuscript that only he or she would have noticed has been eliminated along the way. Yet encountering Monica Ferrell's manuscript, I found it at once entirely convincing. Her poems do not sacrifice the meaningful discovery for the arbitrary or gaudy. Rather, they speak in complex ways because life itself, in all its lived-through moments, is complex.

The poet's imaginative inhabitation of diverse cultural givens, from the Sleeping Beauty tale (in which horses stand outside the tower "dozing, their lumps of maple sugar / spitted with cold"; the word "spitted" so bristles with resonance it stops the reader's breath) to the various animals of chase and table (hart, lamb, lion, human, antelope, wolf) offer evidence of the inexhaustibility of, really, anything—if it is seen with poetry's opening eye. Ferrell's intimacy and originality of perception remind not a little of the power of Hayao Miyazaki's reenvisionments in film. Her poems make vivid what has become dusty, and return us, as real art does, to the brilliance of initial perception—return us, however, enlarged, ripened by all that must be endured in order to see once again so brightly.

Jane Hirshfield

let others vaunt love as they will,
we have love's food, we have the knife!

—Guillaume of Aquitaine

Harvest

I.

Tonight the lares have eaten their offerings.
The sweetbreads are gone, black kidneys
Infantine and nacred as mollusk-eggs. The smoke
Circles and begins to clear.
When the finger points toward us, we answer,
When the eagle opens its mouth,
When the fly sings to a honeycomb
Emptied by plague, the hive scattered with bodies,
Let us not forget the wolf, his last rite.
Let us not forget the due.
These animals bode well for the new year:
We will begin this again and again.

II.

The violence has congealed to a horn, a buck's
Long cartilagineous tube:
It must be the beginning of abundance.
The swarm lifts and banks from the hills;
Everyone is coming to witness me
Coming apart: I have made myself so edible,
So extraordinarily meat.
—The way you spoke to me just now, I almost heard
The murmur of insects, preparing a new hegemony.

We break the glass in the green drum.
The beetle swims in the eye of day.
Time marries me inside myself.

III.

Our witch is lighting the fires; her hut smokes,
Sending up its sole gray plume.
I am homeless. I live everywhere.
The forest yawns open like the ocean, a green grave
Where I could be an intaglio locket,
Birds singing between my bones.
The water-snake slithers in the palace hall.
The blue-white tiles fall off the wall,
Breaking, breaking the Delft plate.
At evening we fished out the boot under the dock,
Scratched our heads and turned home
While the beetles went on breeding there in the boards.

ONE

Geburt des Monicakinds

I woke. A tiny knot of skin on a silver table
Set in the birth-theater, blinking in the glare
Of electric lights and a strange arranged

Passel of faces: huge as gods in their council.
I was the actor who forgets his lines and enters
On stage suddenly wanting to say, *I am.*

I was almost all eye: they weighed me down,
Two lump-big brown-sugar bags in a face
Which did not yet know struggle, burden;

How the look of newborns unnerves. Then
They wrapped me in pale yellow like a new sun
Still too small to throw up into the sky.

It was midnight when they injected me
With a plague; tamed, faded as imperialism, pox
Had once put its palm-leaf hand over a quarter of Earth

Saying, *these.* Now it was contracted to a drop:
And in the morning I knew both death and life.
Lapped in my nimbus of old gold light, my

Huge lashes drooped over my deepened eyes, like
Ostrich-feather shades over twin crown princes: wet heads
Sleek and doomed as the black soul of an open poppy.

The Antelope Chase

In nights of unforgivable lust they slew the wolves
With their bronze-tipped antlers. And now alone they

Rage the peninsula of mourning, the autumn country.
Night burns like the poisoned lionskin.

Your eyes are slits, they cannot cry. Your mouth
Is so full of the dark: you are wordless,

It is before the beginning of speech. Deeper in forest
The hollow chorus has begun, singing scales of lead.

You keep running from yourself reflected in black pools
While the Horned One waits for you, Lord of Beasts.

Walking Home

A cold yellow light on the cobblestones, you
Stumble from the bar, a wayward star
Falling off its chart. October's darkness
Takes your temperature, presses a cool moon
Sliver to your fevering brow. You speak the moon,
Hieroglyphs of jade drop from your stone lips.

Night rises out of the river like a bad Aphrodite:
Jet, burnished as a rococo tomb.
She walks you home, coyly taking an arm,
Dripping her curled locks over your shoulders
As if tonight all your kisses were hers. She whispers
A name into your auricle that turns its cartilage

To bone; she nudges your ball of yarn down still another
Tangle of lit alleys. You pass by the deluging world
Graying in its watery obsolescence, light-strafed,
Where cars sleep the dreamless sleep of steel
And fountains purl like minxing cats, a stirring
Avalanche: the sound fills up the silence like a bowl.

Blue-gray pigeons shatter the air—ungainly,
Deprecating, fatly hurrying to their sick moults.
A thousand minuets lie coiled in a pomander ball
Raised in the pale yellow hall of an Austrian queen;

A thousand minuets lie under the sea
And you too will be one of these, you have only

To find the house in this long row of painted doors
With your number. But the hours spin you on their fortune-wheel
And you walk on, as if one thin bone finger were
Pressing you, a chess-piece through the white and black
Squares of these vacant streets; you walk as the genius
Of yourself—as a shooting star: instant, irresponsibly beautiful,

Without issue. And yet if the good monk should find you,
Guide you up the stair to his tower room, holding a taper
To show you the star chart of all your fatal incidents,
Your sketched-out combinations and imprecations,
Your storied path like ice-skates on the frozen lake,
By morning it would all, all, as always, be forgotten.

Self-Story as Spheres of Egyptian Industry

after a set of models c. 2000 B.C.

I. Cattle Stable

Cattle are being fattened for slaughter; one is so fat he can
no longer stand.

A black mark against the wall where he went down
On his knees, and the man still feeding him,
Hay coming out of the mouth in stalks—
How very carefully he rests on those knees, like a good
Girl holding them, under a skirt, trembling together—
And the one standing next to him, now beginning to scent
His *finishedness*, while in the farther room
All the others face away, poised, about to drink.

The man at the door is crouching; he holds something
Hard, and the door is open, and night,
Night is shining like the end of time
Like the desert contracted to an eye,
And the river rushing so audibly, like the sound
Of his mother rustling softly into a farther field.

> Heart, in this way also did you fatten yourself toward
> your doom.

II. Slaughter House

Oxen are being slaughtered. Another worker is plucking a goose. On
the balcony hang joints of meat.

The door is open, and the goose twists his neck
Until his eye is full of night. His is the pietà:
He the one who swallows and not by wish all
Of the suffering in this room; not the cows,
Lain down and already become clay again,
Nor the men, who, even as they hold the knives
To the dumb throats—see, one already blooms—stiffen
Under the impress of batons in the cricks of their necks.
No justice, in finality? mum the banners of meat
Nailed up, many tongues as one, like a Greek chorus.
Only the goose, craning himself far out while cradled
To be plucked, sees even this is all as the stars have bid.

       So did you, frozen in your bear-trap, stare off
As if, a Medea out of her theater's dug fate-pit,
You could see some solution between the motes of air.

III. Granary

Clerks tally grain, superintended by an overseer; inside the granary
proper, men dump sacks of it into bins.

How they shower it down, the gold of the god;
And this the highest these men will ever rise, ascending
The tall flight of stairs like individual suns. In the afterlife
They will die of hunger: each will lie

With his hollow belly on the riverbank
As the Eastern Ba will with the Western Ba
Become one red bulge blotting out all life.

How the grain is so unaware, it twinkles blissful
As pebbles under the water's clear rinse, like the beloved
Rising from a dream in which she is queen—and for an instant
Half-laughing, asks, *What did you call me?* Before she remembers
And the stone blocks out all light, stopping her up
Back in the cave of *slave* again. For a second: *divine.*

      So did you, my pretty one, set off flying
Toward impossible dawn heights, before you shivered and fell.

IV. Brewery

*The overseer with a baton sits inside the door. Two women grind flour,
later put into four crocks to ferment.*

Behind the wall, the fourth jar is being topped
Off while the three stoppered ones stand
Like extinguished oracles, mouths shut at last.
To be closed up in a black vat forever: is this the way?
Clarifying space until someone with ignorant hands opens
And drinks you whole—and afterward, forgetting it all.
What is the purpose of intoxication when daily
While we grind ourselves under the shining white wand
We swim with both arms through a universe
Just as watery, isolative, and finally speechless as that dark?

10

So for you was there a night when sorrow
Staggered you through the white lit streets, returning
You up the stair to your room: washed out as a ghost
With your handful of vowels, your speak-trap a hollow hole.

V. Bakery
In the bakery, men crush the grain with pestles. The four black ovens are
tended by a man with a poker.

Bald as the beaten year, under the flood
Of soil, blank, black as unslagged basalt,
Their minds are scrubbed clean by industry.
Inside, the little animals expire; their last breaths
Blow up the dough like glass being thought
Into the shape of a goblet. The ruby red heart
Of fire is tiny and we all become
Her someday: we burn still as a soul,
As the opal placed in the blind man's eye.
For now we wait, like this one staring
At the black box of the oven where it all
Takes place. Behind, another man with his back
Turned stabs forward with his pestle as if to row
His bark boat of death sooner to the spread shore.

So did you, under a blue faïence scarab sky
By a cliff wish an instant for that thing which cannot be had twice.

VI. Garden

In the center of the garden is a pond surrounded by sycamore trees.

To be immortal is difficult; add to this
Holy and beautiful and you see our position.
—What small mistakes they keep making, those ones
Who bantered here once, who lay in our shade
And flew off in day like moths. The dream of union?
We *gave* it to them; we whispered it in their ears
While they were sleeping. For them it is still
Dream, a sort of spiral memory, but sometimes it
Passes into life, the way a shadow can pass into brilliance
When the wind shifts. Then is the air filled like genius;
It is almost too much, it cannot be long held.
Don't you see yet? *In our world only is the door shut.*

So on a foreign shore where you came to understand
Joy—your arms full of gladness, it streamed, a fountain—did you,
Reluctantly but choosing it: get up and turn back home.

The Lion of St. Jerome

Out of the fields of Scythia
Came the lion to St. Jerome:
He wanted to learn peace. His gilded jaws
No longer swung open,
Even, at last, giving up
What was not his to give. Then
How the deer rustled in the woods like phantoms
Of his hunger, his heart's desire.

Do not speak of loss without speaking of him.
In the end, to be betrayed by that mouth,
Without speech to defend itself: then he knew
He would never be one of them,
The sons of man. It was never the same
After that. The love had all gone out
Like a bird through an open door
Who will not come back even if you

Call it by name, though it used to eat
From your hand. And Jerome—insatiate,
Torrentuous, inconsolable as a water clock
Eroded by his own secret and terrible need
To love: how he was envious of that lion.
All his life he knew would be wasted
Unless he found his surrender. And that lion shot true.
Who among you would not be envious too?

The Players

All night we played chess. All night we played cards.
I was drunk off my ass. In the cabinet
Teacups shuddered and hid their eyes.

It was Your Move Next. It was Spin the Wheel.
We flipped the dust in the hourglass,
We kissed. Yes, you drew my breath from me

While I counted to seven, blinded. Then how
Brightly the knives must have shined, trying to warn me
Who would kill whom by the end of our night.

Were those dice loaded? Were there cards up your sleeve?
Kitchen flies contemplated me, sadly
And winged past, while the clock's needles got sticky.

My knees shook the table. My neck bled gin;
Cigar smoke floated from my fingertips.
My dear, are you all right? Please: ante me in.

Soon my hotels loomed. Still your houses ran about
Like green ants. Could we *both* win? *I love you,*
I said . . . the silver words ricocheted in the kitchen,

Missed. And so you called bingo, called my blush,
My bluff, poured a hoard of winnings in your lap—
I have never played better, murmured you, getting up.

In the Binary Alleys of the Lion's Virus

Sorrento, your sun is light yellow lemonskin, your sky
Purling out like a farther surf on which I ride away
From that secret in a German town. I left behind
A dragon of enigma to fester there without me, I left
A small god ticking like a time bomb: a tiny jade statue suspended
By magnets in the vulva of a prehistoric temple. Here
In the oyster of your mornings I wake as lead.
                                        Once I was a knight
Who rode out in search of grail, now I am just a husk
Of armor with the gray squid of memory inside—I have forgotten
Land and tongue, I have forgotten everyone. Only I see
An emblem, some kind of lion arrant on ash-argent ground,
A creature I greeted once in a dream: yes, at the crossroads of the
    hallowed grove
He kissed me—and must have slipped this curse between my lips.

Stories from the Tower

1. Sleeping Beauty

Now I have been asleep a long time.
I am grown opal, unbreakable: a white blade
stretched along the bed. Out my tower window
all the animals are arranged
like frozen jewels in the snow: the horses
dozing, their lumps of maple sugar
spitted with cold. And the birds, nodding
on the line, full of fairy slumber. In life
they will not know such peace again,
such absolute rest. They are swallowed whole:
feathers tucked in stillness, hearts like a coal
become unburnable in this world.

I am suspended
in my error's ether: what business did I have
trying to spin my own thread?
This is what is meant by *fate*.

2. Her Rest

At night: the snow. Always this unvarying
deepening. No sound, no wind, no life:
I am not yet dead. Nor sleeping.
Ask for a sign you will not get one.

17

Ask for time the bottom drops out
and steadily unravels, an uncontrollable
white thread unspinning the winding-sheet.
In my cedar chest the folded gowns
turn over and sigh to each other,
lost in dreams of breezes belonging to spring evenings.
Once I could move where now it is all mind,
all solitude. Nights like this it seems impossible *he* could make
a difference. Even the steps have surrendered to be stone:
There is a kind of vacancy too immense to ever melt.

3. Prisoner of the Golden Cage

Now, in this blue room, we will give ourself
up, let the long siege go, like a fist
opening to find the crushed bug flown.
Come cousin, it is the hour of surrender:
let us not say it is not so. Snow
is falling on the mosque, is falling
on the gold dome. I remember
lessons we received at the hands of the Master
who pinned butterflies to the enormous page
and turned it. Once there *was* something here,
but that was a long time ago, another world.
Please don't be angry: the sea is singing
me to sleep, the water pouring its green
poison into my ear: *earth ends, earth ends.*

Nighttalking

As I lay down in the echo of the day
The moon became a brazen mirror.
The sun became a lion grazing under earth,
Memories grew wings like flies and clouded here.

No one but the dead understands me tonight,
They've put their blue hands to my marble mouth.
They murmured among themselves and checked their notes
Then at last decided to leave without speaking to me.

Darkness, when you place your hand on my forehead
What do you feel, sickness or that fever
Lifting from me as the lake clears of fog?
I would like to be useful as these springing streetlights

And unbreakable as my kitchen knives.
I would like to be wound very tightly, like
A mummy made of gold thread coiled around
Some wax statue, which inside is let to rest and heal.

Queen of the future, I will wake with amethyst eyes
When the moon has finished with her witching.
Then all the gold lights of heaven will fall in me like seeds
And sprout marvelous trees, drooping with heavy love.

At the White Quay

I.

Blue-lidded, I woke at dawn
With my mouth full of moths,
I blew them up and was free of them,
Free as a harmonious sphere
Shrunk to the body of a girl, white-armed and pure.

Like an angelic presence the window glowed:
It was the future, hot and incandescent
Calling me to its lip like the open
Hole at the end of the cave calls
Wondering Lazarus.
                    Then
With my hair dressed, my lucky blue
I took the seal of myself in hand
And left the room.

*   Could anything ill . . .*

II.

Night, the portents of a dream
Came out of the cauldron:
Ill, ill, ill.

I paid the pundit overtime.
He pulled them out like hot towels.
Ill, ill. He shook his head, I paid the pundit again,
I paid him with my fat wallet of tears. Ill, ill, ill.
My hour ended.
               So I woke with the pale
Light a crescent on my face,
Still in my bed pure as a virgin saint's
Fingerbone in its white silk reliquary.
If only I had stayed. Dressed there in light
Like a feather in a temple of linked hands.

But I shivered in the mirror: my lip burning
With a dreadful fox's grin.

III.

All the lindens whispered, *Go back*.
The churches afraid to toll:
Huddled together like old women.
But that tipped
Ball-bearing on its greased track, the impetus of the thing
Floated out beyond us
Out of reach.

If only I had listened to things: at every turn
They tried to tell me.
The doorknob, the telephone
In its glass booth, hovering

Gloweyed above me like an older sister.
This is not for you.

                         Yet how it's true
Time keeps its cards close to its chest;
Then at the last instant, very carefully
Lays down one you've never seen before.

With my hair dressed, my lucky blue.

IV.

All night, the valves of the mind
Pumped language between the twin black bags;
I ran the hamster wheel, the dream of me.

Old wolf under long-missed skies,
I scented those familiar hills
And howled my whole first story,
The clear wild notes fell like stars.

Now I understand what Ovid means:
A thing we do can change us forever
Imprisoning us in a shape we never meant to be.
Anima mutandis, the frozen tree; the barking beast.

22

V.

I woke at dawn, my resolution cold
As a silver pistol in the bed beside me.

Shadows passed bluewhite on the street:
The dissolve of the modern city.

I washed; I dressed. I checked my reflection,
Wavery as one already beginning to disappear.

Today you are acting a tragedy
A girl has grown sick of her happiness
And overturned her plate, she wants to read
The verso of the world.
                                  Then like the one
Lowering herself into a dry stone well,
I kissed a Trojan Horse, tonguing that whole
City of night.

VI.

For three days, half out of mind, I set
The iron clock to my ignorant ear. *It barely breathed.*
Old noble thing: what kind of world is this?
I assure you, you hardly want to live in it.
Even I, the bearer of your beating body
Do these things bequeath. *And then*—if you believe it—
He gave up his tick. I could not weep

But turned back to the tinker shop
Where I was welding together a terrible robot.

All the sisters holding their faces in bowls
Of laughter, as the Mother Superior counts down the row
After the Devil's been for a visit.

VII.

After the parcheezi
He sets his hand to a yawn. We shall play
Again, of course. Tomorrow, of course.
We shall play until the black bull's blood flows black.

      For I am so vast, my mouth
Encompasses you as the universe
Takes a star. But, bizarre,
Babylike in swaddling blankets
You're the unkillable Zeus, Krishna, Moses—
In a year I nixed all the other kiddikins
Yet you survived, o prophesied plague,
Blight in the Pharaoh's wheat fields.

Holy Nile, extinguish this living unbeliever—

VIII.

Yet the river
Was beaten like bronze,
The river
Lay perfect armor,
Pouring through its stone artery like a century
Following its white general.

A queen without powers (I
Gave them up—)
I chatter
Like a parrot. I jump up and down:

The tied jester
Left on the shore of depravity.

IX.

O world, I am smaller than a chip of opal,
Hardly valuable as a river of blood.
I weigh the oars on my arms, I am a fly,
Not a scarab with its claw of eternity.

On the bank of the ocean of suffering I poured
My whole sorrow out, until I was chaste as an urn.

As the Eyelid Protects the Eye

Tonight, I might approach you;
That's possible. Might creep over the ocean,
Whose gray-blue waves would bend to my foot
As they bend to any good purpose,

And slide myself down your street,
Up the steps to the room where you are sleeping
In the striped sheets. Down beneath the skin
Of your skull right now dreams are sweeping

The way water sweeps in the shallow edge of a pond,
Dark and murmurous, amoral; untrustworthy,
But you don't know that. You let them drift,
Take pleasure in the sand they raise up, swirling

As if it were anything more than that,
The simple play of what is deathless
Because it has nothing to do with life.
And when I drape my invisible gauze

Body about you like the metal apron
In an x-ray chamber, don't be surprised
How they fizzle out like moths in flame,
How their supernal voices go speechless

As beast-barks, so that helpless choir disbands—
Because it would have been for this only
That the moon held steady her milky flashlight
And the waves went lead as I crept from my window,

That the granite of gravestones tightened
In expectation, and even the flowers beating
Like time bombs in the soil paused, breathless
At the event. Everything in the world knows

What you are too asleep to see. And wants
What you do not wish for now, tossing in transparencies.
Everything with life in it has my love
For you purled inside it like a strand of hair

Which, when plucked, releases volumes of feeling.
When I arrive, you will be like the sick girl
Of whom Jesus said, *She is not dead, but sleeping.*
With my fist on your forehead, my lips at your neck.

Myths of the Disappearance

I rise like a red balloon, untethered and vacant.

The essence of my dolor has become rarefied,
Holy; like a fragrance, bodiless, without referent.
It is a pale shadow on the sun, a wasp's-wing, accidental
Splash of poison on the white rose's thorn—
I twist it in my fingers and faint. *Shall I tell you?*

There was one bad fairy at my birth, there came one curse,
One blister, one drop of mercury in the moult of me
And everything was ruined after.

                              Still it is
No good; the words drift from me like ashes.
I am so old now, I have left half my life
In caves hollowed out in rock by the seashore:
I prayed in each one, and could not find my way back,
Or lied when the pass-word was asked, or turned my back,
Making gestures of despondency at the roiling surf.

            In a mirror I shot all my hateful selves, the yesterdays.

TWO

Mohn des Gedächtnis

Picture it: a girl in a strange city
Unpacking her suitcase, setting things on shelves
In the middle of the folds rises the berry
Of her determination, a black pearl on white cloth
As fine-wrapped as a baby Jesus
Or new star—she the one who will set it in the sky
Tomorrow, it's only the night before still. Picture it,

This stranger: doer of an incomprehensible,
Resonant past thing, which echoes in the oyster miles beneath.
Who *was* she? Some figment, miniature self,
A toy soldier set in motion by
An accidental kick of the dreaming real girl,
Far away untouched and unblemished in sleep.
Yet I was she: I was the eunuch who, smiling, salaaming,

Lets in the ghostly sahib to the huge jewel room
While his hukkaed shah lies fallen. That night,
A little doll stuffed tight with my fell purpose,
How I wandered the city, outdated treasure map to hand,
Searching my buried gold. Where my fear went
Skipping a few paces ahead, a paper butterfly, later
I hung my tears like earrings from the lampposts.

—No!

I could make a thousand poems from this,
There came in one day enough pain for ten
Natural lives laid end to end,
I could make a whole galaxy of glowing suns
Heating their decades of planets and trash—
But how can I let this live through me any more? Or
I should be the girl of the music box:

Open her red coffer, out
Pops the same old song,
Only magical for never changing,
Crystalline, distilling
Its own liquor of eternity
From the sole inexhaustible god-grape—directing,
Suspending me as the magnet-chip in the old jade statue.

Now I may lie tossed up by this ocean, like an old
Jellyfish losing its clarity, hexed
By a curse ancient as a blue faïence
Scarab carved with hieratic marks,
But even if it means a change as came
To Anthony, after the god abandoned him—
Human, no longer tragically, singularly destinied—

I will live through *it*: burn it up
With my breath. For after all I am alive
While what is past has lost that art.

Echo Digression

Who is she who difficults my steps on this path,
Overturns the stones and makes strange signs?
It is the dead one, it is the shadow-bag
Filled with ash and wax parings, bloated, huge

As a termite queen ceaselessly spitting
Out the poison of a lifetime in eyeless infants.
It is she who lies on me flat when I dream,
Squeezing me free of breath so that I wake up

Gasping; she and I correspond, we have the same
Knot here in our left chests so you can tell
We are cut from the same blasted tree:
The grain of one's wood never changes, you see.

Now my knot widens like an eye and so does hers;
These two black eyes stare at each other
And wordlessly speak, planning terrible things—
Well, I am not afraid of dying: this chess-square

I occupy will long be mine after I am iron, or tin,
Or whatever cheap metal they choose to make me in
When, little idol, I will face their suns like a worshipper,
Be stationed toward the east as if I wanted more of this.

Myths of the Disappearance

I am the one black-eyed and rabid dog in the king's pack of elk hounds,
Drooling and dripping with bitterness. When he blows his horn
I foam like a hypocrite.

—*Enough*, girl-child, you have talked yourself into a fever again

Let us sit with our radio and favorite tunes, alone in the old house
While the hurricane winds shake the casements like a child
Demanding you avenge yourself.

Eleven Steps to Breaking up a Hart

> *"Stop, in God's name! What are you at? Whoever saw a hart broken up in this fashion?"*
> *"That is the custom of this country. Are you versed in the art, boy?"*
> *"Yes, master," he replied. "The usage is different in the land where I was reared."*
> *"How so?" asked the huntsman.*
> *"There they excoriate a hart."*
> *"On my word, friend, unless you show me, I shall not know the meaning of 'excoriate'!"*
> *"Dear master," answered Tristan, "since you ask (and if it will give you pleasure) I will gladly show you my country's usage, so far as I have retained it."*
>
> —Gottfried von Strassburg, *Tristan*

I. *Tristan, the boy so far from home, removed his cloak, placed it on
   a tree-stump, and rolled up his sleeves.*

Dear One, it is seven years this summer.
I have counted them out. I write you now
To say the thorn we thought removed has
Festered, and spread its gangrene in the blood.

I loved you once as one loves a star
Which cannot be spoken or called
Though one keep one's name for it
Under the tongue: that private, interior name,
A genie in a bottle.

I trusted in you as one trusts in a pear:
That it is a fruit; that it wants
To give itself in sweetness.

II. *Those present eyed the boy with ever-growing interest.*

Not here, but in that other country
You taught me the meaning of *merciless.*

I was delicious: I was still soft inside
And you hurt me like a pearl.

Come, let us tour the rooms where I bottled you
And strung the tiny vials round my neck

Where they banged against my collarbone
To drown out that other drum, the red one.

III. *After making an incision he slit the creature from the muzzle to*
    below the belly.

You taught me
Longing;
You made me
Mortal.
And for this we remember you alway
In our Lord's Prayer.

IV. *(This is the way to break up a hart. Those who know how to*
    remove the breast are sure to leave these ribs on it.)

I apologize for being indiscreet, but you see

The body of your betrayal
Has just washed up on shore,
Like a beached whale
Moaning to be quartered, eliminated some way.

V. *Thus the hart was dismembered according to the rules of the*
   chase. He laid the breast, sides, and quarters, both fore and hind,
   in a neat pile on one side. With that the Break-up was over.

You left me in a snowstorm on a glacier
Netted with crevasses
And took our maps.

I froze before I found my way back home.

VI. *Tristan, the young master-huntsman, was ready to oblige as*
    before. He took the pluck (I mean that on which the heart is
    strung) and cleaned it of all its appendages.

Do I repeat myself?... Do I begin to bore?
It is the stuttering sickness,
The banshee drowning in the same old well.

VII. *The company closed in and inspected his huntsmanship.*

Outre-mer, in that Holy City,
We traded pictures of our truer selves:

But when, afterward, alone, I opened mine
Your locket was empty. Then
How I raged like a prince cheated of his kingdom
Or magician throwing the glass emerald against the wall.

VIII. *This done, he summoned the hounds with a loud "ça, ça, ça!"*
They were all there in a trice, standing over their reward.

Now I live among others
As the mermaid did with her fisherman
All those years by the sea
Sworn never to reveal she is a witch

Or I am an apsara
Who, coming back from her bathe,
Finds her skin-sheath stolen
And must go bodiless through the world.

IX. *"It is a beneficial practice," said the eloquent youth, "since the*
bits one lays on the hide serve to flesh the hounds, the blood
being sweet to their taste."

When you came all the way to my imagined palace,
Climbed the spiral stair to my tower,
I thought you had come to release me:
But you took my secret treasure and locked the door.

X. *"Now take your hide away," good Tristan continued, "since I have*
   done all I can. And believe me truly, could I have served you
   further, I gladly would have done so."

Surely you know the legend
About deer:
Their eyes are not like human eyes. You see
If she is still alive
When you cut her open, if the walls of her heart

Collapse like a besieged city, then
Her last picture,
The image of her killer, will in those amber pools
Be frozen
And carried down with her into the afterlife.

Sacrifice

How softly they blew into the lamb's dark hooves,
Whispering love into those four small listening voids,
Before they skinned and strung him from an invisible hook,
Where he glistened white and rose like a baroque sunset
Under the guillotine, a rare splayed beauty of
Sinews and blue rivers like an unseamed continent,
Or the delicate veined porcelain of a Fabergé egg
Pried from the cold and phthisic fingers of a nobleman
Incapable of letting go: after he left the best part of himself
In a room across the sea he never went back to,
Dealing out the remaining decades of his life
Wandering the four chambers of the heart,
Now and again fluttering his curtains open
Against the same, unmerciful landscape.

In the Grips of a Sickness Transmitted
by Wolves

Sorrento, at night the long fingers of your orange lights
Prick me in the sizzling streets, where the pinnacles
Of other people ring tinny and papier-mâché. Is this the way
Up to the murderous cliff? it's most important that I get there
And leave no witness. Is this the majolica medallion
Which marks the grave of girl abducted by a stallion
Whom she gave a lump of maple sugar?

                                    For that was in an autumn,
The time of year when young girls get hopeless and feel like
Giving it all away, the way a matronly merchant
Might brush off her lap, at the iron end of the market day:
It's over, it's worthless, without deserving and without
Purpose have I nourished this hope in my small patch of earth,
A sickly weed whose nodding sun's gone nova.

Myths of the Disappearance

You have stolen my joy from me. Why should I lament?
The church-walls sweat blood listlessly,
The horse shudders in his paddock and moans.

You took my joy from me, the way a cat
Steals the breath of a sleeper, or an incubus
Defiles the shieldless body in the vault of night.

And now I ride the slim line of this disappearance:
Like a wire of radioactive metal,
It slices through time and space, it is without place or fellows,
A fishing line
Trawled out endlessly to catch what it cannot know or wish for.

I am the magician's ruse, the floating signifier
In the floating city of fire.

Paradise

I. *The garden of Eden. Also called* earthly p.*, to distinguish it from the* heavenly p.

First

She is seventeen, he twenty-one.
She is a green girl, Ophelic but believing
Herself a witch-queen, while he plays Edmund,
Bastard and natural. Sitting on the cliff's edge, her
Back to the village where floats down the sound
Of wild clog-dancing and the cars of old women
Driving their drunk men methodically home,
She thinks, *I want to be like everybody else,*
To hurt and love: I want to be human.
Cue him: in the darkened theater a wisp of hair
Tickles her ear like a whisper and she is
Enchanted. Steal her right off if you can.

II. *Heaven, the abode of God and his angels and the final abode of the righteous. (Now chiefly* poet.*)*

Moonlight with its beautiful scatter of white lies . . .
On the hill we pass among wrought-iron crosses
Where people died in roadside accidents: you explain
Just as I decide to commit my own for ever.
Waving fields of hay as if for the yearly sacrifice—

The goddess is shaken and rises distraught,
She is not what she was. It is freezing in this dark
House put together like a coffin not meant to last
To the Resurrection: when we shall recover all
We have lost, sea-beasts spitting up their swallowed
Arms and legs and voices. . . .

                                        What is that noise?
My unhappiness.

                                        What is that noise
                                            again that noise—
My unhappiness unfolding even unto heaven.

III. *A place like Paradise; a region of surpassing beauty, or of*
        supreme bliss.

Sure, come, you say, *for maybe, two days?* I
Don't understand yet but I will . . . in lovely Oslo,
The hair of people are full of light, their skin, their eyes
And it is the White Nights so even when we walk
Home near midnight the world is luminous.
I think I could stay this girl forever, a record
Spinning around in this kitchen singing you
This song; I'd watch you slowly change as the sun
Watches a tree grow or a balloon regards the little
Giggling boy who lets it go . . . an inch-length Buddha
Is trapped behind glass at the Viking Museum;
But how did it *get* here? *I don't know,* you grin.

IV. *An oriental park or pleasure-ground, esp. one enclosing wild*
   beasts for the chase.

Now let the universe explode
                                        now let the ship of nails
Sail in, now Balder has received his death-blow
From the "harmless" mistletoe: see, he dared them try
To hurt his impermeable body but the trickster
With the gilded tongue found out where he was weak.
My mouth fills with rage like a cave with a thousand bats
Shitting their magnificent guano—but all too late,
For now in the dozen frozen attitudes of naïve agony
The fawns in the forest of my heart find they are
Shot down and turned to stone like these statues
In Vigeland's Park where it has just begun to rain
And I stand motionless in the pose of loneliness.

V. *A pleasure-garden; spec. the garden of a convent.*

Here in my cloister, I have you. In the city
Of ladies, in the courtyard of language
I immemorialize you. How does it feel to be
A god? Nero said *sweet, sweet, sweet as honey.*
I place your name sparingly on my tongue
As the Eucharist, and I don't share it
With anyone, making a new monica for you.
Finally one night I drink eleven clear stars, then
Open my mouth and vomit forth your story.
Little secret: you have your own holy books,

Pages of my diary, scriptures and interpretations
As if you were Kabbalah and I ordained.

VI.   slang. *The gallery of a theater, where the 'gods' are.*

From this distance you appear small, more like a puppet,
I can see where the joints of your mouth
Ride up and down, such a clumsy wooden nutcracker
I grow suspicious as to who's been on those ropes
All this time. Ten years gone by—now I find you
Horribly shrunken, like a cannibal's prize skull
Down to the little chit you first were. So: it was *I*
Who blew you full of air, as a glassblower shapes her vase
Pinching the film into your expensive face. Thank you,
Thank you everyone; the part of the dead girl was played
By me, the part of the dog by the dog. Goodbye.

Dormition

Tonight you're alone in a way that seems final.
Stars grow arms and turn like the seeds
Of dandelions blown on or octupi floating in their
Own cold dark without coordinates. At this hour

Each cup in the kitchen has the white, open mouth
Of a dangerous lily and you want to drink from them
One by one. You will take your time, the way a stripper
Takes off her clothes to stand draining there like watercolor.

One pictures a dancer getting fainter, closer to trance's
Black door at mind's end. One imagines the feeling
Of snakes in a basket growing still as glass,
Children who stop crying suddenly for no reason

A Fabergé egg winding its battery down.
The moon trapped in that lake.

In the Gabinetti Segretti

after the room of sexually-explicit frescoes from Pompeii in the Museo Archaelogico, Naples

What is simplest is before you
all the time, in any room, the intimacy
passed between two people like breath,
like the golden mirroring between
a lake and tree and lake:
none of which is original, but reflection
folded in many pleats as water,
as a smile floating up willless
from happiness when laughter is startled
out the way a bird takes sudden,
spotless wing.

On all these walls, still living, peach
and yellow and burnt red: all to describe
the intensity of his gaze as he draws
her toward him, as if actually saying
I mean this all the time. And she cannot
be frightened: everything is pulled
so clear, the time for fear is over,
it belongs to that whole other world
now reduced to a droplet dimly
there stirring then vanished,
a dream in a deer's eye.

Now all the sky shivers with storm
clouds and as if someone is taking
her, very carefully, into a barn; ducking under
the low door's lip, she trembling at the hand
and along the skin—it is almost
like an Annunciation, light lasering through
the body to that hidden eye in the chest
and opening it. How can it ever now close?
Leaving the blue shadows of the barn,
the world will be new with rain:
white, wet black branches, irretrievably

alive. Someone has touched that sole silver string
in her and plucked it—it startled them both
with a sound that had never before been heard
only *heard of*, like a bedtime story told then forgotten.
And this other one, here on the opposite wall,
he is nothing if not unpeeling, and so rapidly,
with such brilliance and no stoppable
momentum—and *she* taking it all in, making
sure there is nothing of him left outside,
nothing left like a dog

in rain at the back door, no particle
of his inness—as when a candle burns straight
through its good wick, not a speck unlicked
by the pure tongue of flame. And I, to think,
I wandering all this time, practically on my knees,
through disbelief and the more terrible
belief, raying ever straight like a targetless

49

arrow over land and sea and toxic, salt-cursed
vaporous nights after what can be found in a place
as four-walled and small as a heart:
contained in one plain room.

Myths of the Disappearance

Let me, why not then, why can I not: be?
Let me meet the vision on the surface of the water—
The leaf falling to its twinning on the river—
The angels shouted at her birth, they gave her a name,
A melody, they pressed a white-fire tongue into the still
Unfirm chambers of her mind, they slit open her eyes.
Why cannot I be the girl I was made to be?

Ha! Your so-called *real* you is an imbecile
Fanatically trapped behind the unfindable opening
Of a stage curtain. Great Scott, with everything handed to you,
Given to you, cannot you find your way out *now*?

Presently
The boats will row away by themselves,
The magic vehicles;
Choirs of birds, fleets of dolphins will
Rock away from me, even the groves of
Yew trees turn their backs, and the tapestry
Knit itself a new ending, a broken
Girl on a greensward by the black flood's rim.

You have painted yourself into a corner
And that corner is closing, with you stuck inside.
Now relish your kingdom of arrogance, your disappearance.

THREE

What Is the Night

I am hidden as the one approaching,
The list of questions slit in the granite slab's
Erasure, and your slow swallowed last word, stolen
By your new stone tongue. How well they heed me,
These keening women in the hull of the sinking
Burial ship, where I linger as a moth on the eyelids
Of the one who will softly waken. I am the cloth
In the mouth of the lion-headed god and the adze
Of his five killed cubs. I am the forgotten sacrifice
Remembered on the boat's return.

Not the rose but the rose's stratagem, its sweet
Guidance into the dark maze where it kills the bee;
I am the last flare gun dropped in the ocean, the empty
Oar-sockets knocking against its sides as the boat
Enters the blossoming storm. I am the breath
Swollen in the lung of jade, the bald gray
Tooth upturned by the farmer's hoe. There are
No ghosts. There are no dreams which cannot be
Explained by indecisions. I am the deluge rising
To the antique stores, with the cats trapped on the high

Shelves inside: how there they purl and murmur.
I am the rustle in the silken pavilions, and
Of the ambush at the river: I am its *too late*.
I body the ruby's dream in the fire—at last

It is all mind, it will not bear child. With
The dawn, I am the two burning sides
Of the bed on which the fevered girl keeps
Turning, of the coin which the gambler persists in
Throwing, but alone I am the footsteps
Of the one who is approaching hidden.

After a Rest: Palimpsest

The violet silk stretched taut against the sky,
the church-bell melody ringing me slowly
awake, like a lady from the sea
dreaming on her cloud of foam, the branches
of the tree all leafless now, entirely
black and slim so that it is visible,
its arch like a hand, a vase full of holes
like the soul, that holding yet penetrable thing—

And everything in me has been collected
during this sleep, and by this sleep's own
volitionlessness. As if I were a vial
in which the perfume fogged, then
condensed as its rare liquor: I am so full now
of the shining chains of years, the change-
self who met the same name-definition
each time with a different bird, monkey, petal,

clasping and unclasping fickle brook, thorn
sharpening herself in slow silence to a point
then widening to the wordless sea.
She is the ten-thousand-faced girl and almost
scares me, flashing through woods like the White Stag
dazzlingly a step before her pursuers;
or she resembles these gladiolae. How
even on the same green stalk, some are just

opening their moist skirts and wet-lashed eyes
while others have begun to huddle, ringed
like ash-tinged cathedrals, like a woman in whom
bitterness has risen to the lineaments
and is all anyone can taste,
including her. How heartless it can seem:
this pink one, for instance, drawing first breath
despite the one below falling now into a swoon

which will only deepen as the world's
footsteps grow more and more muffled, never less.
And these new ones, slender as Gothic towers,
not even touched yet in their tight green cases—
are they believing right this second in that tiny
spot of blue they will see at the tunnel's end?
Will the vision of my ceiling be enough for them,
no actual sun, breeze, far from their singing
sisters, separately going through the twelve
stages of age, as life walks up their stalks
like a finger unzippering a dress—it falls
breathtakingly open, on the floor, and warm—
Even cut from their ground, these long slim
necklaces of blooms prove metamorphoses
insist, constantly altering, superseding faces
into palimpsest. I cannot be afraid of my future.

Knut Hamsun's Night of Fire

Afterward the maid came in with new sheets,
Her face smooth and polished as a moon:
As the pewter mirror of a pewter jug.
She knew everything and understood nothing.
Fru Janson sent up a beaker of water; I
Threw it out the window for ice.

The curtains were so beautiful, my God; it was
Like being enveloped in velvet and rocked
To sleep. It flowered like a lady's hair, like the sigh
Of coming-undone, all arms, white thighs—
And the lily-throats of angels, tiny, rising,
Invisible, no voice, all mind, shining.

Nowadays they tamp out my light
With their little silver thimbles, it fizzles
To nothingness. I wanted to swallow the whole
Vial of genius because I was dying slowly
Of their snuffers. Do you know how that feels?
Like a moth blurring in a bowl of milk, stirring

Fainter, fainter—fainter—becoming whiteness.
They thought they'd tame me, top-hat, three-piece
Suit, the life of significant fruit. But I am

A wound, blooming red through everything, like the curse
Of the jar in the disturbed mummy's-tomb: I am desire
And desire's matchstick. *It didn't hurt at all, you know.*

Kaisarion

He was not tricked. Kaisarion
Turned back to Alexandria, to where
Her barge stilled the river. Must it be ruse
To step into the mouth of this? Death
Laid lightly, a white sheet
Over the body of desert.

I. Berenike, the New Constellation

When the fisherman had finished with the rigging
and tucked their brown, believable hands
and their brown, realistic faces
back inside their white gowns, back behind their
rows of nacreous teeth,
the two messengers appeared on the pier.
How serious the eyes of men here, passing
in the street at evening, walking gravely
in the dusty alleys by the market.
—What are they hurrying to? Under the failing light,
slipping through the nets of shadows,
something is speeding them forward, something stands
at their center,
like a black, unliftable meteor.

I shall never be married.

II. The Point of Departure

At sunrise, fish are still sleeping in the sea.
I like the cool of it, the sweet-pink-pure,
enfolded as a somersault; possible.
It shivered me down
stone steps, to where our caravan was waiting,
my litter like a gold mouth
under inexorable blue. Sleep and Death
took horse—or so I like to call them:
I know all of Homer by heart, I learned
my lessons well. Mother said in Rome
the most important thing to learn
is *perceptum morior*: learn to die.

III. "The Club of Those Who Die Together"

Let us not forget that in the month of May
she sent me away from her forever.
I am outcast;
I was the only one.
And then she took the jasper, ivory, jade,
she took the lapis, obsidian, carnelian,
agate and closed the door. How can I save her?
I am too small not to float
on the wash of this
enormous refluency.

62

IV. The Eye of Eritrea

And in the desert the sun
is a lecherous uncle
fondling you in your sleep,
his fat red paws
opening the webs
between your untouched limbs.

Lie still.
It is better if he thinks you don't feel it.

V. Philometor

Not here, but in another life
she was a swan, and I
her white star,
precious and fated.
I was the snake-egg
that does not hatch:
a perfect circuit,
curved, immaculate, and full of promise
surrounded by her heat.

VI. The Tutor Bribed

A sum
accidentally left on the slate.
A clapper
fallen out of its bell.

I am a shepherd asleep on a mirror in a mountain
as his whole flock crosses into the Summer Country.
When he dreams he has found his brother
clouds pass overhead,
showing him a trick of light and air,
an enormous hoax.

VII. Alexander, the Invincible Seed

I know where they keep the corpse.
She took me there.
He was not *deceased*,
he was ruined:
translucent and terrible
as a massacre between stars.
And the lady, the lady
with the green face
kept chattering in the shadows,
they say she makes him live forever,
they say she gives him breath
in the other world.

How he rested, as a poison
sleeps in the veins, irremovable,
quiescent,
before it starts blackening the heart.

VIII. Protected by Pharos

These armies she drew to Egypt
like a dark magnet, a moon
sodden by toxic waters,
lost in the alleys of her city.

IX. "King of Kings"

And when they made me a man,
when they made me Caesar's son,
I hung my head and stared at the ground.

Those are wrong who say
she never cried. Mother:
I am coming, I am one hundred
white rats
leaving the river for your forest.

X. Coptos

I am lucky like this:
my days are inverted, these
cities file by in reverse,
I will die in the city of my birth.
Coming we had to fight her all the way—
now the Nile is drifting me toward it,
downriver.

Everything can be taken back.
Even oracles lie.

XI. Death Without Weapons

Night
shakes me like a tambourine,
sudden and irregular—
This fever is sewn into me,
a red thread in my binding,
the magic cord.

I have stayed fatherless and foreign
like a word no one can pronounce.

XII. Under the Uraeus

The way she died, on a Saturday
with a small marked mound
where I used to feed:
bluewhite, a double Venus,
balanced scales,
red gate
into her marble heart, darkened halls
where all victors sit, crowned with lilies.

If I could live there, even
as a statue, a garden ornament,
mouth of a fountain that will not close—
cannot speak
for giving—
I would, Mother I would.
I would live there
if you would let me in.

XIII. "A Plurality of Caesars"

The bottom of the river is tar.
The core of the world is black.
If I want to I can swim
under all of Africa,
I am His only begotten son,
god.

So I will give myself up.
I will flatten this body and its blood
into sand.

       If the body of the desert is raw, a wound
like the sun unpeeled, blistered:

The soul is a solitude that can go on forever.
It has no friction
There is no loss

Alexander Leaves Babylon

Alexander wept in Babylon, not because
his father had died or his old tutor
had looked at him finally with those eyes of stone

but because the drink of Babylon
was so good. It tasted of dandelion milk
squeezed from a stalk still in its greenness.

Here in his hand—the world: but first this glass of clarity
swelling like sunlight and as sharp. Yes, winter
had aged him suddenly as a straw statue left outdoors

in the everness of the terrible Gedrosian:
that skin-colored bowl soft as the palm of God
where the urge to understand met the urge to disappear

and the two lay down to couple in the dust.
Sand scrubbed him clean as a glass there; he came out
empty as the strange room that widens between

two heart-beats: vacant as this circle of faces gathered at table—
flames staring quietly from a white fire
visionlessly patient in its dinner of elimination.

I need no one else I am a star

Then the gemmed
cats ranged under the table, and a rainbow-
colored snail kissed the marbling foot.

Herculaneum

How the boys on their motorbikes pass staring—
Little silver hooks which miss their marks.

This ash-covered town stinks of fish and olives,
Rank purple flowers which drip down from the trees

Wide eyes whose dark gaze creeps along my skin like beetles.
Wouldn't it be wonderful if everyone had a mouth like that

Dried fountain, an enormous, outrageous rococo *o*
Which orates only its own wedding-cake frosting.

Were you zephyr in your former life? that blustery wind
Of which this dead town has lost all memory...

—Flat, flat, someone lay me down a new
Round of cards, I have nor aces nor queens,

Have nor hearts nor arms, only a mouth with this
Emberish volcano dangerously aching at its core.

Now the aisles of bees want to lift from me
Their gold army tiers, winging away toward tomorrow

And I am voiceless in the garden by a marble bench
Where the barbed-wire fence pricks my fingers as

If I could fall backward now in some Sleeping Beauty trance,
Have a hero catch me with his kiss—ah, that old insipid wish.

The Fire of Despair

To flux the snakebite I swallowed the whole
Vial of venom. Presently, vapored and fevered, I
Became the queen who lies on her lion-footed couch
Sweating into the light white sheet of day.

—Everyone is whispering behind a thin screen:
They speak of her *pulse*, her *signs of vitality*, her *blood*
Pressure, the awful bolus of its squeezing
Far too much red stuff into far too small a pump.

Now the fires are all gone out. For three days I have been ash;
On the fourth the slightest wind can blow me to pieces:
A scrap of a smile, shred of the has-been-girl clinging
Like remnants of a sail scattered on the blank sea.

The soul is a number moving by itself

It is not cold at the top of the stairs.
The years strike like radium drops.
There is a little door, there is a little lock,
There are many good machines whose purposes are lost.
In the plump and tidy cabinets
The red drawers are full of numbers
Irrational and fatly simpering,
While the white drawers have numbers
Imaginary and drifting,
And I am one of those.

Oh, the furnace wheezes, the charwoman sweeps,
The wood sighs and settles and the dormouse sleeps.
Don't try to look at me directly.

Drink

for A.I.

That endless chapter, like a long corridor where leaves
Fall at your heels in autumns you hardly notice,
And by your sides the tight green whips of spring
Unspool into whites and yellows you barely see

Except to tweak another brainish fantasy,
Champagne-colored clouds backed like a whale or rabbit
Blocking out the sight of anything but your own
Hands and vandalized mouth while the mist closes you in.

Ten years ago, you moved in a fogstorm on a glacier
Latticed with crevasses and put your whole soul, like an orange,
Into the palms of God's chance; without residue.
It was a beautiful thing to be pure: beautiful

But heavy as a gold pendulum dangling on its cord;
How your hands itched to cut that filmy rope—
Once in a taxi you thought you'd burned up to ash
Everything that mattered: but when you woke the next

Morning found a new paper flower folded in its place;
Once by a sea you thought you'd spit up the last
Of your good genie: but as you turned to sway home
Its singing swam over you just the same,

Opening your mouth, you heard the fresh clear notes
Come floating out golden and even forgiving you...
Dive after dive into the inconquerable black
Spat you up high on an unapproachable rock to croak *Saved*.

Dizzy as an initiate who tries to hold in the holy
Mouthful of dark blood he has swallowed, you've patiently
Clawed for years—your rats' teeth have gnawed until
Their gums are bleeding, yet it hangs on its sinew still,

Tremulous lantern, shining dimly in Alphabet City
Where you dredge for those lost overboard
To these reckless years: and its faint light guides you
Derelict, errantly late to some singular birth.

Homecoming

How you greet me when I return to bed
where you are soundly sleeping: you
somehow hear me, sense it in your sea-depth
and rise up opening, folding back the white
down quilt—still sleeping, entirely unaware
of the motion your clear heart is making
through the agents of the body—and then
you kiss me back into place: almost as if
smoothing my hair, you kiss me back
into the indentation kept ready by your hand
searching the island of its true rest.
That you do all this so I may slip
soonest into mine, that these two are actually the same;
and that when I am like a girl asleep in a dream
of herself in a dream in a dream of herself
as a Russian doll with its many selves, you are the one
who comes to kiss and so dissolve them all:
I've never told you; how I know about us.

In the Rain

In the rain I stood a leaf detached from its tree by the lake
where I waited aimlessly for your face to appear in the rain.

You were always golden, a shower of insignificant things,
I a Danae, coiled up yet somehow powerless against such rain.

When you talked, words spilled from your mouth like a herd
of flies black, green and shiny as a branch just washed by rain.

Once I left my room, shut the door, wore my green child's slicker
so I could come to your house and say, *Please let me in from the rain.*

What did you think then? Your eyes flickered like eagle's beads
over me or the dice of eager men licked by spit or an indifferent rain.

Then the door slid back on its root and I entered among clocks
and papers to the porch with its ashtray and tin cup filled with rain.

Those are the tears of the world, you said and laughed—as if it was funny:
I think perhaps you have never stood outside all night for someone in
   the rain.

I think you have never watched a river, say the Hudson, and seen those
lights floating on the water and known your dead were now rain.

You are simple as the child playing with his india-rubber ball, while
I am the darning-needle of this story, borne down a gutter by rain.

Sit down, you said, a grinning death's head. *You must be frozen*;
with cold x-ray vision you saw my skin where it lay soaked with rain,

all those hollows of breast and bone, shivering in pricked gooseflesh
that unlike the goose's was never meant to perfectly dispel rain

nor let me take a few steps off from you and saying nothing
but some inarticulate cries fly sorrowing away in this rain . . .

Well: those are the kinds of stories that make you yawn and gloat,
kinderlieder for those still amazed by the chthonic power of rain

to sway our moods and mimic our tears or bring forth an enormous
unwarranted heart simply by feeding one rootwork with its rich wet dark.

Harmless, Recalled as a Fairy Tale

After our rendez-vous—this the last word he said,
Waving to me as the train pulled away from the station.
And so it seemed: harmless. Till evening brought
The first prick of fever, which soon trellised my veins;
At 2 AM came that knock on the city gates,
Little pig, little pig, let me come in. . . .
Ha! ever a bold and warlike people, we didn't.

Days of siege. We threw corpses dead of plague
From the tops of parapets to frighten it away:
But what *was* it? That vatic voice was not like his at all,
and by its speech one could tell it somehow knew us well.
The mystery deepened. A strange billowing cloud
Made my people short of breath, I heard them wheezing.
The end seemed near. What could this ailment be?

Hunting out clues, I went over the roses and snows
Of his departed face like a treasure map, over
His words hanging in air like the scrolls of Alexandria.
Had I not been consensual, a free agent,
Gay, single as any singing lark, who
Chooses what to unlock, to whom? Well?
One night, finally, I climbed our tallest tower, lay

In the open on its roof and had a brilliant dream.
I saw my body nestled between angels

Like the body of the prophet Jesus, I saw it
Leaking from a finger's tip like a slit ragdoll.
And then I saw: this feathery, amorphous creature
Black as mildew in the bath, soft as bread mold,
Chewing on my bloodpuddings in the corner.

And then I knew! That morning, I went out by the porter's door
Pressing one finger to judicious lips like Oedipus.
Your name, I said, *I have it now: Despair*—
Shrieking, it vanished with brimstone and flames.
So I etched *Harmless* in that ground of merds and moss
And to this day, my people listen to strangers crying wares
With an intelligent ear, remembering our grave old danger.

The Blue Grotto

Somewhere in this world I will understand
that room: a *natural heaven*—the *personal
swimming hole of the old Augustus*—:
What a beautiful crock. Yet
how the boatman swindled us so gently;
we hardly minded. And then—
the violence of the sudden chain breaking
            us into the splendor of a new life—

We idled on eternity, out of time.

I stood up in the boat
holding out my arms like a chick
burst from its white shell,
one low blue blaze in an ocean
of blue fire.

Life was full of struggle.
All the struggle of this last epoch
was not over and would not be over,
was a rare sweet wine in a crystal phial
pressed from hours of rain sliding
down in streams the mind's train window
to be drunk on a day like this, in one straight delicious draught.
So my heart was broken: it would break again,
but my tiny muscles would stand it and my bones

as long as I stayed willing. *Let me stay*, I prayed,
pure: unapostate and without deceit in the face of being.

Then the boatman began to sing, he rolled
out the opera and the salty local,
he told tall tales and ludicrous jokes
and I laughed. Here, at the end
and beginning of my voyage. For this, this it is:

The island where your name is unhidden
and now you must leave it
as we must leave everything perfect until
we enter that great wide sea.

Somewhere in this world I will understand my life.

Notes

Geburt des Monicakinds—"Birth of the Monica-child," after the medieval German painting title "Geburt des Mariakinds," "Birth of the [Virgin] Mary-child."

Self-Story as Spheres of Egyptian Industry—the italicized section headings are excerpted from text accompanying models exhibited at the Metropolitan Museum, New York.

The Lion of St. Jerome—A wild lion joined the monastery of St. Jerome. Wrongfully accused of eating a donkey in his keeping, he was taunted and banished by the brothers; when, through a lucky accident, he was able to prove his innocence, they invited him back again.

Prisoner of the Golden Cage—Younger brothers of the sultan of the Ottoman Turks were imprisoned for life in a room in the harem, called "the Golden Cage." They were expected to assume the throne in the event of the sultan's death but frequently died or went mad in captivity.

As the Eyelid Protects the Eye—the title quotes a phrase in Tolstoy's *Anna Karenina*, tr. Richard Pevear and Larissa Volokhonsky, Penguin Classics, 2004.

Mohn des Gedächtnis—"The Poppy of Memory," after the title of Paul Celan's book *Mohn und Gedächtnis*.

Eleven Steps to Breaking up a Hart—the italicized material at the top of the poem and in the section headings is excerpted from Gottfried von Strassburg's *Tristan*, tr. A.J. Hatto, Penguin Classics, 1960.

Paradise—Balder is the name of a Norse god who was able to withstand any weapon except the humble mistletoe (a fact which the trickster figure Loki manipulated to destroy him). At Ragnarök, the Norse end-of-days, various destroyers of mankind will sail in on a ship made of human fingernails. Vigeland's Park is a sculpture park in Oslo, Norway. The italicized section headings are excerpted from the definition of the word *paradise* in the Oxford English Dictionary, Second Edition, 1989.

Knut Hamsun's Night of Fire—"Then my passion broke out in other ways: I took to loving light. I assure you, it was an absolutely sensual love, a carnal lust. . . . I never understood Nero's delight at the burning of Rome until then. In fact I went so far as to set fire to the curtains in my room one night." (Letter to Erik Skram, 1888, published in *Knut Hamsun: Selected Letters 1879–98*, ed. Harold Naess and James McFarlane, Norvik Press, 1990.)

Kaisarion—Son of Cleopatra and reputedly of Julius Caesar, Kaisarion was endangered after the defeat at Actium. Cleopatra sent him east, intending him to seek asylum at the Indian or Persian courts; he made it as far as Berenike, where his tutor, apparently suborned, is said to have lured him back. In Alexandria, Octavian, who could not tolerate the existing "plurality of Caesars," had him strangled.

Alexander in Babylon—Alexander the Great died of a mysterious fever contracted at a feast in Babylon. He was there returning from his campaign in India; it had ended with a disastrous crossing of the Gedrosian desert that gruesomely decimated his army.

The soul is a number moving by itself—a quotation from a passage in Aristotle's *On the Soul,* where he parodies the ideas of other philosophers.

The Blue Grotto—"La grotta azzurra," a celebrated natural wonder on the isle of Cápri.

Jerry Bauer

The Author

Monica Ferrell was born in 1975 in New Delhi, India. A former "Discovery"/*The Nation* prizewinner and Wallace Stegner Fellow at Stanford University, she is currently an assistant professor in the creative writing program at Purchase College. Her poems have appeared in *The New York Review of Books, The Paris Review, Tin House, Fence*, and *Boston Review*, among other magazines. Her first novel, *The Answer Is Always Yes,* was published by The Dial Press in 2008. She lives in Brooklyn.